Studio Sergison
Accademia di architettura
Università della Svizzera italiana

Autumn Semester 2010
Modernism as a contemporary vernacular (1)

Contents

This document is part of a year-long study undertaken by Studio Sergison at the Accademia di Architettura di Mendrisio exploring Modernism as a form of contemporary vernacular.

The city of Tel Aviv was chosen as the setting for the first part of this study for its remarkable urban fabric. The 'White City', which was designated as a world heritage site by UNESCO in 2004, boasts one of the world's finest collections of buildings from the early period of the Modern Movement.

Our work considered the status of the city's urban fabric and the contradictions implicit in the preservation of the urban legacy of a movement that had itself advocated a break with the past.

As an economically dynamic city with a growing population, Tel Aviv needs to consider the potential for densification and rebuilding within its exisiting urban fabric, but this requires difficult forces to be reconciled.

The students worked on a number of sites that are under great pressure to be developed and studied building proposals that were deemed appropriate and realistic. The sum of these works is an attempt to define a conceptual framework of our studies and offer a positive contribution by addressing the difficulties and dilemmas the city faces today.

Typical view of Tel Aviv, showing the layers that document the transformations that have occured over time

The history of twentieth century architecture is invariably written in relation to what became the dominant tendency in the architecture of the period, notably the Modern Movement. The evolution of International Modernism has been extensively documented and is the subject of one of the most comprehensive bodies of theoretical and critical examination in architectural history. For the sake of clarity, I use the term Modernism in this paper to refer to early Modernism, rather than later revisionist forms, such as Postmodernism, that treated history with a degree of cynicism.

In the simplest terms, we know that Modernism was partly born out of frustration with the limitations of classical architecture when called upon to offer adequate solutions to specific twentieth century building needs. It was also the result of the socio-political impulse to offer more universal solutions to housing needs that expressed a sense of utilitarianism and innovation. The Modern movement attempted to break with history and the tired academicism of the classical method, although this had already been achieved, to some extent, by German Expressionism and Art Nouveau. In the early 1920s, a number of ambitious young architects felt compelled to propose a radical new architecture that championed a simplified form of expression that with connection to historical precedents. This was their claim, and it is certainly one that needs challenging. The contradictions that emerge in the rhetoric, however, do not detract from the effect it had on the way we now think about the recent history of architecture.

Arguably, the two documents that best encapsulate the position of International Modernism are 'Vers Une Architecture' by Le Corbusier (1923) and 'The International Style' by Philip Johnson and Henry Russell Hitchock (1932). The authors of these seminal books were not necessarily the originators of the movement, but the documents they produced communicated the ideas of Modernism in a manner that elicited broad interest.

In their book 'The Heroic Period of Modern Architecture', the English architects Alison and Peter Smithson catalogue and record chronologically the early period of the Modern movement and the work of those they later refer to as the first generation of Modernist architects. Never missing the opportunity to reflect on their own future legacy, they did not question how the first generation's work would be considered by future ones, but rather how the work of their own generation would be judged in the fullness of time. Many of the examples the Smithsons refer to are without doubt the seminal buildings of the early Modern Movement, the so-called 'heroic period'. We all know them; they have been widely studied and interpreted and have been incorporated in what we could call 'high architecture'.

Today early Modernism is considered a period of original and creative thinking, and much that followed was produced with reference to the work of the early Modern masters. The second, third and whatever generation of 'modern architects' we are up to now, are working with known solutions or types. These seminal examples of architecture produced almost a hundred years ago continue to influence architectural production, and underpin the pedagogical approach of many schools of architecture. The projects documented by the Smithsons were the subject of careful study and interpretations by subsequent generations of architects, and the Smithsons themselves declared their own affinity with Mies van der Rohe, Le Corbusier and many others on numerous other occasions.

The extent to which the historical European city can support or frustrate an improvement in the urban condition was widely argued. In some instances, Modernist urban strategists referred to the possibility of creating a utopian city. It is important to recognise that much eighteenth and nineteenth century urbanisation created unsanitary conditions, with grandiose public buildings standing against the backdrop of the miserable living and working conditions endured by many city dwellers. Their impulse to act on the city in a bold way that might improve the lot of its ordinary inhabitants is therefore understandable, even noble. We know now that it was the Second World War, rather than architects' arguments that allowed the realisation of large-scale urban projects. However, the historic centres of European cities have remained largely intact over the course of the last one hundred years. There are exceptions, of course, but nowhere have urban ideas alone been the only cause of change.

It is necessary to look beyond the European city to see the Modernist urban aspirations realised in the most complete and, arguably, purest form. The cities of Chandigarh and Brasilia are attributable to a number of visionary architects, but Le Corbusier, Oscar Niemeyer and Louis Costas are generally credited as the authors of these very ambitious urban projects. Both of these new cities were unburdened by the need to compromise an urban vision in response to strong topographic constraints, or in order to absorb a pre-existing built fabric.

The same cannot be said of the two largest cities in modern day China, where the historical building tissue is considered only as an obstacle to the unprecedented growth of a modern city. Shanghai and Beijing are the embodiment of the Modernist doctrine, in their systematic demolition of entire neighbourhoods over the past twenty years: very few buildings dating back more than fifty years remain today.

Up to this point I have attemped to sketch out the background and consequences of a Modernist attitude, whose advocates wrote passionately to communicate their ideas, in a rhetoric that admits little sense of doubt.

The words 'modern' and 'contemporary' are very closely related and are frequently used as virtual synonymous. The Oxford English Dictionary (OED) defines Modernism as 'a style or movement in the arts that aims to depart significantly from classical and traditional forms, a movement towards modifying traditional beliefs in accordance with modern ideas'.

Proponents of the movement believed traditional forms and beliefs should be questioned, not as an ambition but as a possibility. We know that Modernist architects turned to industry and mechanisation for inspiration: the image and structural organisation of airplanes, ships and grain silos excited Le Corbusier. Since the early period of Modernism, architects have been exploring the possibilities of mass production and the standardisation of components to improve construction efficiency and economy and the egalitarian impulse that inspired them resonated with certain forms of political thinking. High-tech architecture, which is another facet of International Modernism, is obsessed with this approach and fails to recognise that the building industry stubbornly remains low tech, as well as largely inefficient, and in fact it is hardly what one would naturally define as an industry.

If we now turn our attention to the word 'contemporary', which the OED defines as 'living or occurring at the same time, belonging or occurring in the present, following modern ideas in style or design', we can see an implicit connection between the notion of being modern and being contemporary. As architects, we need to be careful in using the word 'style', as it refers to an image rather than an idea. This is part of the difficulty in relating the word 'design' to architecture, as it represents images of things rather than a concepts that have an intellectual ambition.

The ambition to be 'modern' has survived for a hundred years despite recent claims that it is time to abandon the Modernist project. There is, however, much compelling evidence that interest in it is far from exhausted, and the many interpretations of the canon of Modernism have proved remarkably resilient. Indeed, in the context of twentieth century Swiss German architecture, Modernism can be seen as an uninterruped project that continues to inform contemporary practice. In certain cases, a revision of pre-Modern references occurs, but these are always in relation to or tempered by twentieth century knowledge and sensibility.

We now need to examine what we mean by the word vernacular, which the OED defines as 'architecture concerned with domestic and functional rather than public or monumental buildings'. This implies a local, regional way of building, that derives from practical constraints and empirical experience. Although some have tried to reproduce the vernacular in a contemporary and very delibate manner, it is not possible for architects to construct a truly vernacular architecture. It is inevitably a contrivance because the vernacular cannot be constructed in a conscious manner. This does not mean that contemporary architecture should not be of its place, sensitive to local conditions and circumstances, but it is difficult to understand, given the capacity and potential of the contemporary building industry, why it would make sense to build today in the same way that was practical and appropriate in previous historical periods.

This is not to deny that there is much that is difficult and, indeed, contradictory in the set of decisions we need to negotiate when we argue for a form of construction that is appropriate to contemporary needs. This is one of the greatest challenges architecture faces today, and partly explains why so much recent architecture is spectacularly bad. What is interesting, however, is the extent to which the Modernist programme sought inspiration from certain traditional or vernacular building forms. I am thinking particularly of the voyages made by Le Corbusier, Kahn and many others, and the influence that the domestic architecture of the Mediterranean islands (particularly Greek) had on the emergence of the pure, white and simple Modernist or functionalist architecture. By looking to the past and the primitive, an answer was found as to how to appear modern.

While they do contain their fair share of buildings that may be categorised as 'ugly', many towns and cities in southern Europe have fully embraced the Modern movement and its potential to realise and build in the manner that its early exponents aspired to one hundred years ago. When looking at a city as large as Athens, which is relatively homogenous in terms of its architectural expression, density and urban structure, the result is indeed impressive. There are many other examples of towns and cities that continue to build in the idiom of modernity. Many of the individual contributions are, if not remarkable, often decent buildings, which have an urban dimension and good internal organisation.

This is what the implicit contradiction in the title of this paper alludes to: the possibility that a large component of contemporary construction, while conforming to the rules of the Modern Movement, could be understood as a form of vernacular: Modernism as a contemporary vernacular. How the building production of the last fifty years will, and indeed should be treated in another fifty years' time remains to be seen. There is a paradox in the current status of the modern buildings that are considered the best examples of their kind, and include buildings that are less than 40 years old. An implicit aspect of the Modern movement is a rejection of the past, which is at odds with the current trend to preserve all that is considered to be culturally or historically significant. In our age, the pressure to preserve the built fabric of contemporary cities is increasing. Buildings that were conceived as having a very finite life are now protected by statutory powers in a way that is at odds with modern architects' strongly held view of the future of the contemporary city. The Barcelona pavilion and the Pavillon de l'Esprit Nouveau epitomise this paradox in that they were destroyed and then rebuilt, so that they now exist as reproductions of the originals.

Le Corbusier's work often had a prototypical character. The same cannot be said of Mies van der Rohe's: the rebuilt version of his Barcelona pavilion is an imitation of a masterpiece. It is ironic that many modern architects tend to advocate a view that is unsentimental, until the longevity of their own work is in question.

We now turn our attention to the large collection of buildings built in the 1920s and 30s in Tel Aviv. While they cannot individually be compared to the seminal, pioneering projects of early modern architecture, taken as a whole - as a city - they are remarkable. No other city can offer such a large-scale example of a humane urban settlement built in the idiom of International Modernism. Casablanca is another notable example, but it does not equal Tel Aviv.

In 2004 the area referred to as the 'White City', i.e. the part of Tel Aviv that was most substantially built in the 1920s and 30s was granted World Heritage status by UNESCO. The municipality of Tel Aviv views this status with both pride and frustration.

The masterplan drawn up by Patrick Geddes for Tel Aviv in 1928 was conceived as an urban project that would take ninety years to be realised. The pressure the city faced in the 1930s and 1940s to house Jewish immigrants fleeing from persecution in Europe resulted in it being executed in a considerably shorter time than originally anticipated. As a result, it was realised in a manner that closely reflected Geddes' ambition. It is likely that without such unexpected pressure, periods of reflection and questioning would have led to a diluted version of the original vision. Instead, the area of central Tel Aviv was faithfully built in accordance with Geddes' masterplan. It is important to note that this plan employs the logic of a grid as a means of organising the city, although not in the dogmatic manner exemplified by North American cities as Geddes adopted a more picturesque urban approach, incorporating garden city ideas.

Tel Aviv exists today as a paradoxical urban condition. On the one hand, it exemplifies the potential for building a city in an extreme environment. It is a relatively low-density city, easy to navigate for visitors - and remarkably green. Many of the buildings realised are well-planned, decent attempts to provide solutions that are sensitive to climatic conditions and socially responsible. While UNESCO offers recognition, it does not offer financial support to ensure that buildings are appropriately maintained, and as a consequence the Modernist legacy in Tel Aviv is now in a fragile condition. The atmosphere of decay that pervades it is an expression of the difficulty in investing in a future that is far from certain. Some would also claim that this character is a quality, and that it would be lost if all buildings from the 1920s and 30s where immaculately maintained. The city would then become a museum, rather than a living city, in much the same way that the great Renaissance cities of Italy would be lost if every building was 'restored'.

Tel Aviv is a working city, which is facing pressure to accommodate ever more people. Currently the municipality is allowing a number of significant high-rise buildings to be erected particularly along the sea front, and permitting older buildings to be extended. The combination of these possibilities threatens the survival of the Modernist legacy.

But Tel Aviv is not alone in facing these pressures. All developing cities must find ways to manage the tension that exists between the need to allow and control expansion and the desire to preserve the existing urban fabric. The definition and balancing of these priorities is the focus of contradictory claims and remains a challenging responsibility.

A street in Tel Aviv

1
The impact of traffic in
contemporary Tel Aviv

2
The sea front

3
Tel Aviv as a garden city

4
A residual plot used as a car park

5
A tree-lined avenue in central
Tel Aviv

3 4

5

1
One of the sites selected for our investigations

2
The Hornstein house: An example of the early period of the Modern Movement

3
Typically fragmented urban tissue

4
View of Tel Aviv and the sea

5
One of the sites selected for our investigations

6
The 'White City' of Tel Aviv

4

5 6

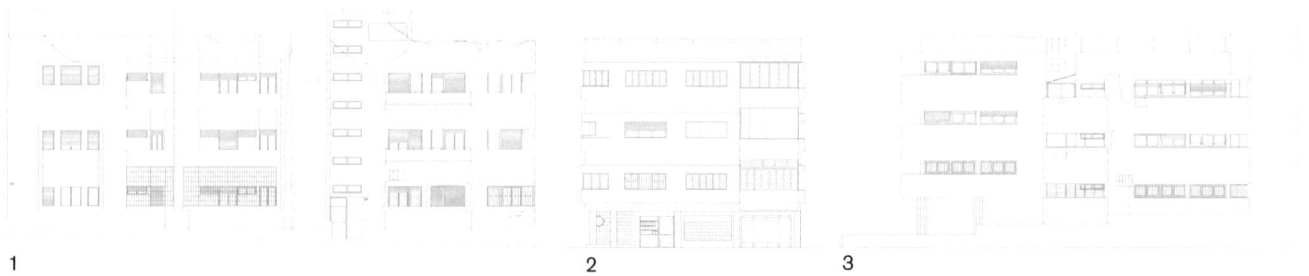

1

2

3

1
Anne-Dorothée Herbort
Mostovoi House
Guela Street

2
Marco Leite Velho
Maison Guttermann
81 Ben Gurion Boulevard

3
Serena Santini
Victor Nagi House
3 Mapu Street

4
Alice Dolzani
Maison Engel
84 Boulevard Rothschild/
Rue Mazeh

5
Eleonora Geminiani
Aginsky House
5 Engels Street

6
Chiara Zunino
Yarden Hotel
130 Ben Yehuda Street

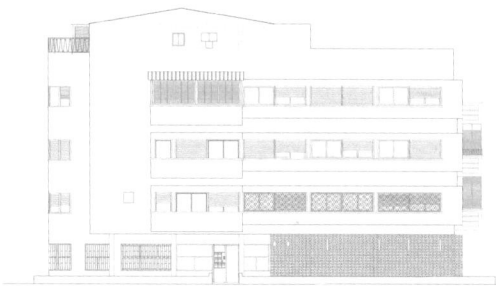

4

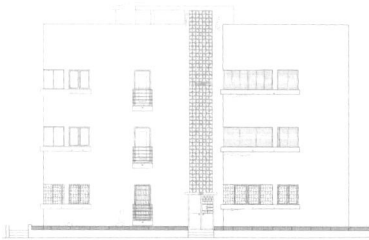

5

6

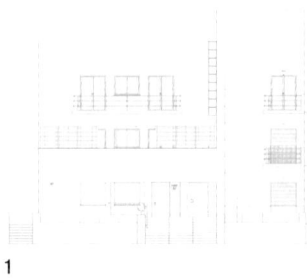

1

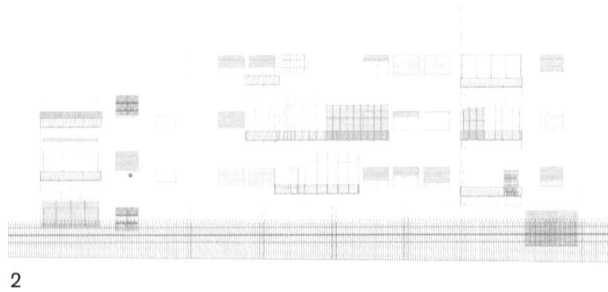

2

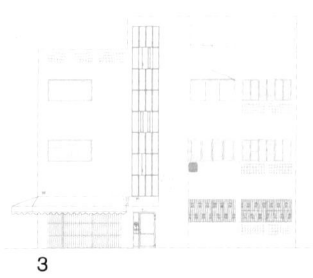

3

1
Mara Bardelli
Schillman House
57 Ahad Ha'am Street

2
Marco Leite Velho
Me'onot G House
Reines and Spinoza Streets,
Ben Gurion Boulevard

3
Florence Harbach
Efroni House
95 Ahad Ha'am Street

4
Natalie Oren
Arlozorov House
6 Belinson Street

5
Elenora Dalcher
Belilovsky House
Gordon Street / 80 Dizengoff
Street

6
Alexandra de la Chapelle
Baumol House
87 Boulevard Rotschild

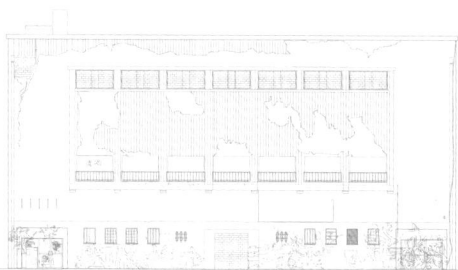

4

5

6

Projects

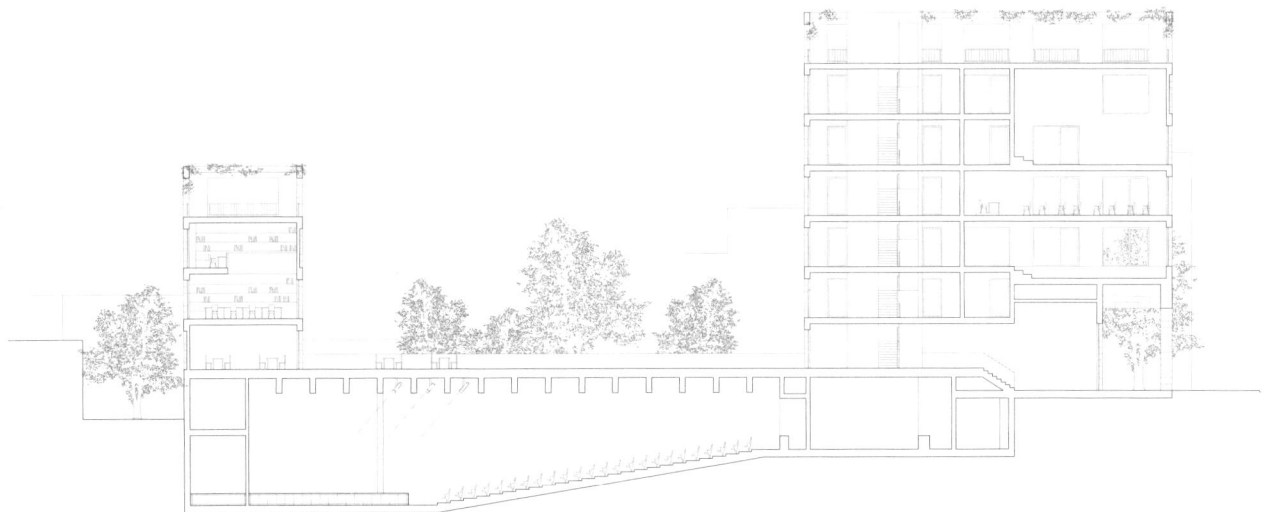

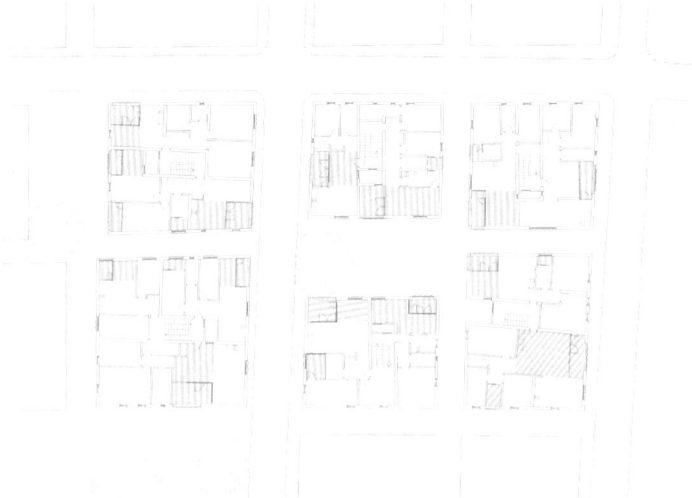

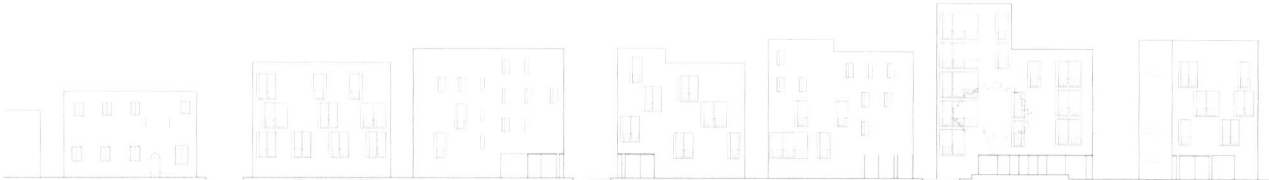

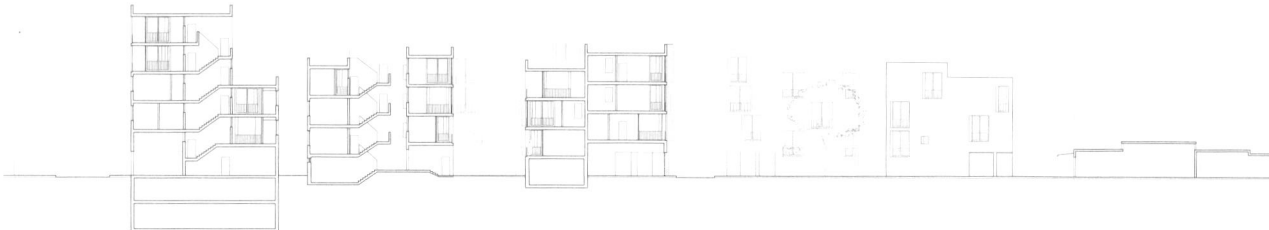

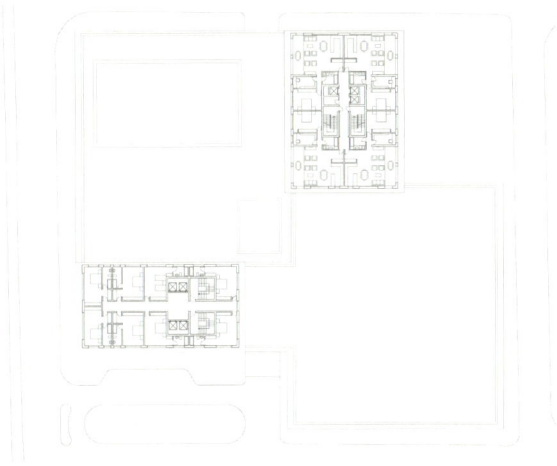

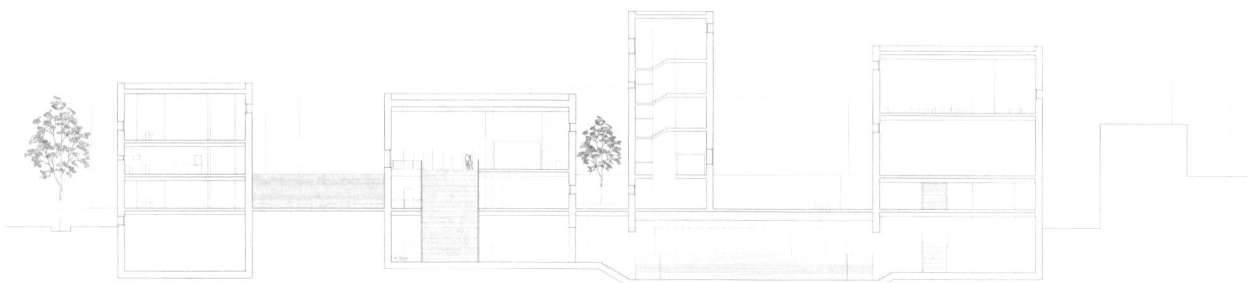

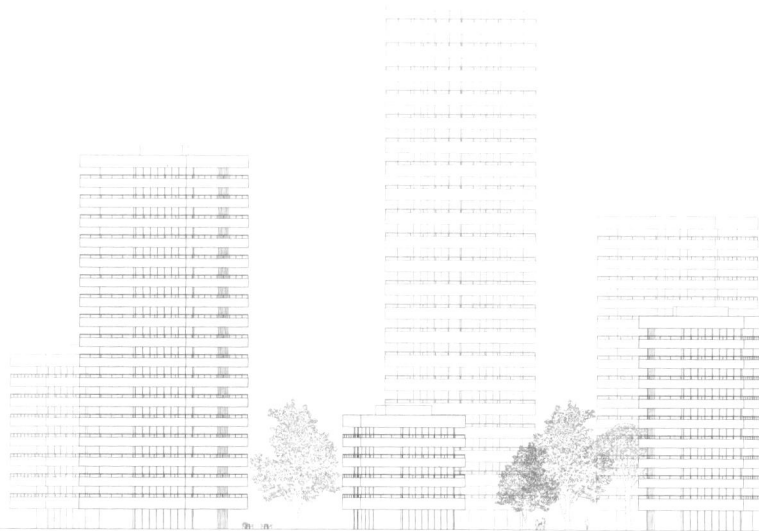

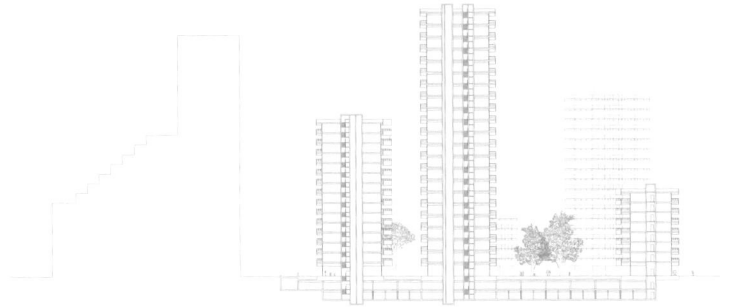

33

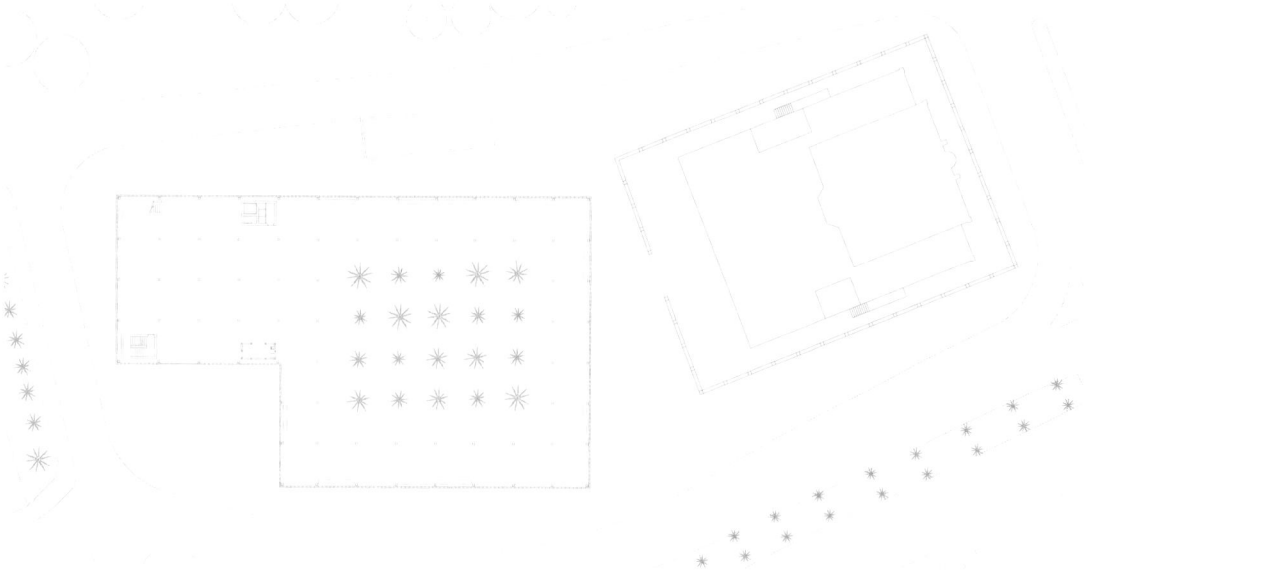

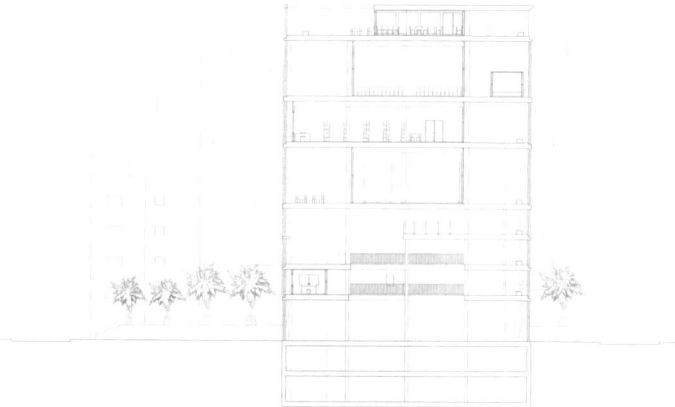

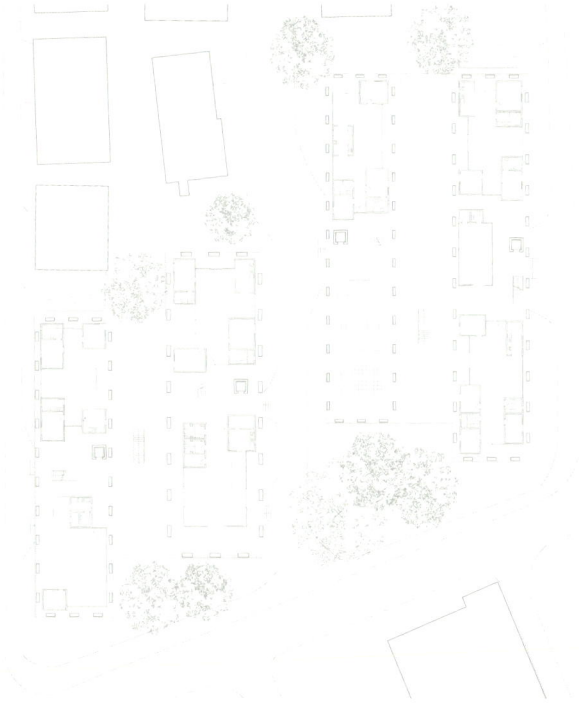

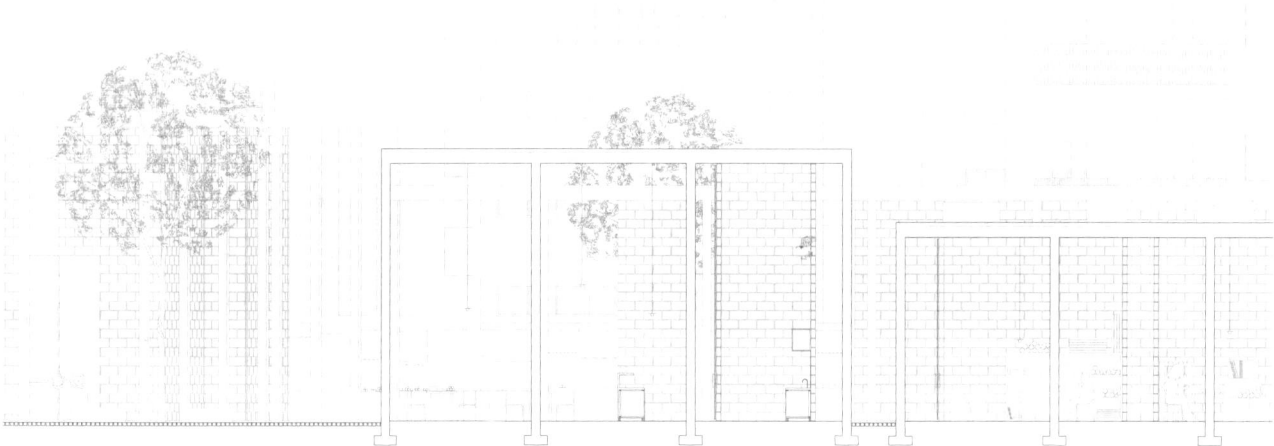

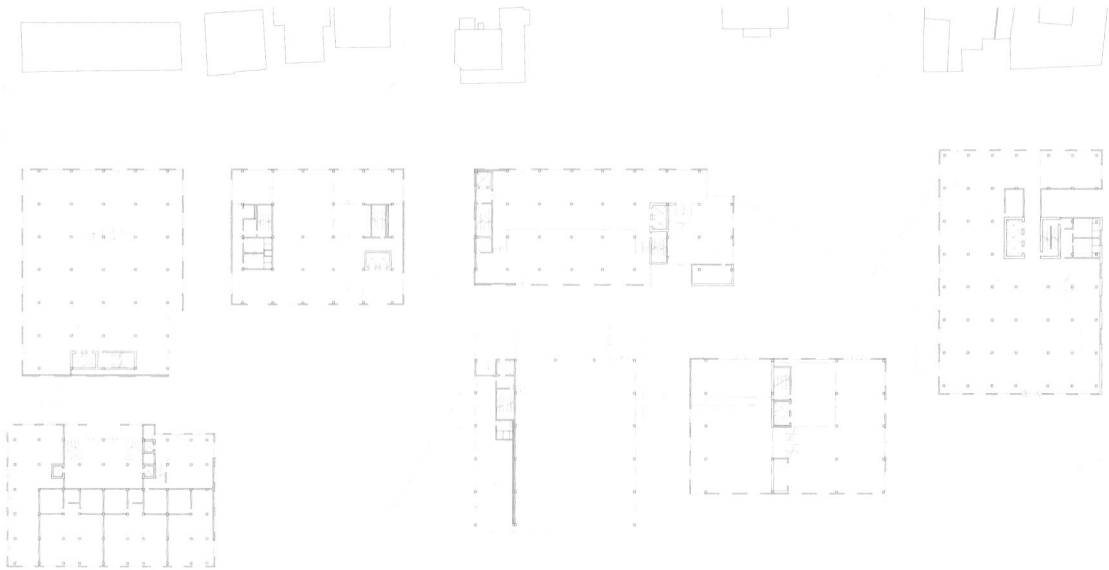

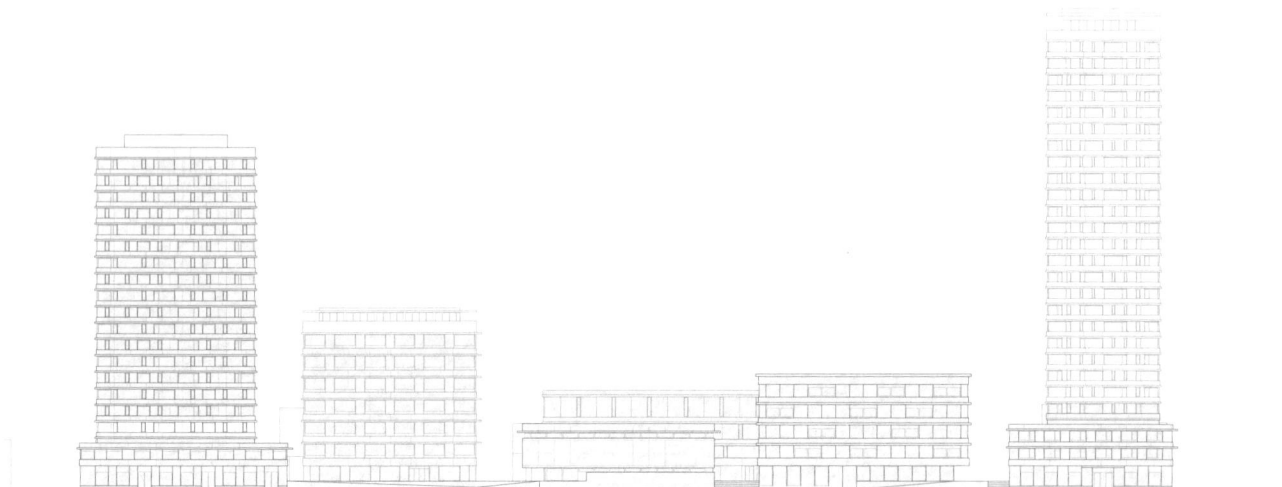

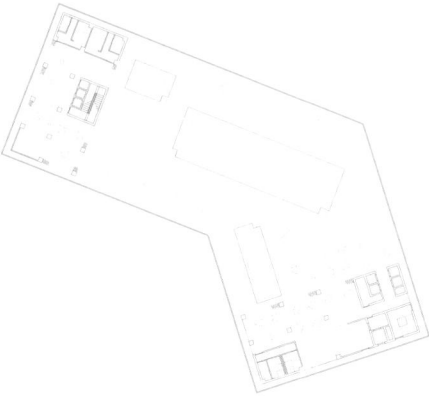

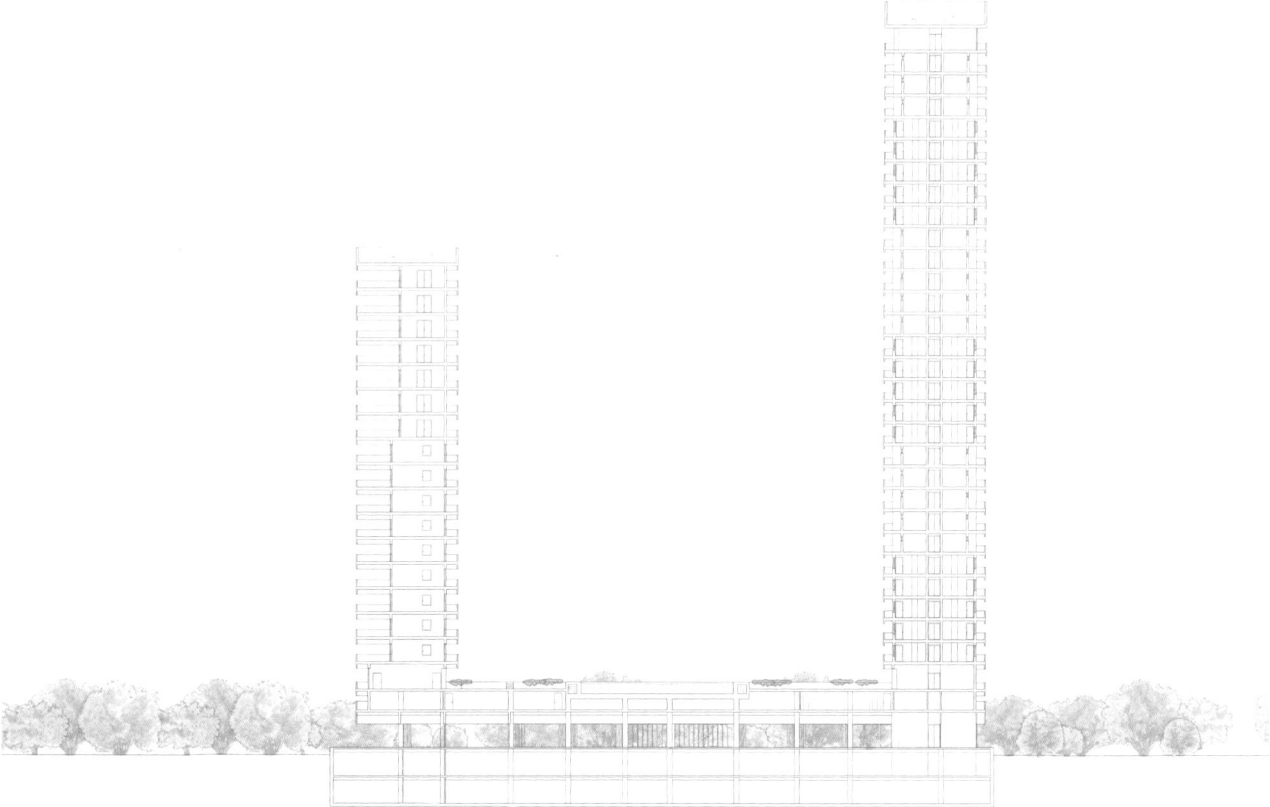

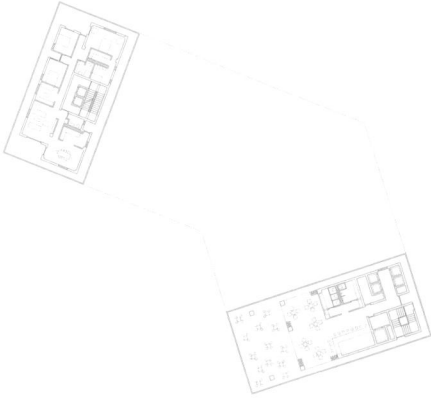

Catalogue

Alice Dolzani, Serena Santini p36-37

Clara Alfieri, Eleonora Geminiani

Mario Marino, Ruben Valdez p40-41

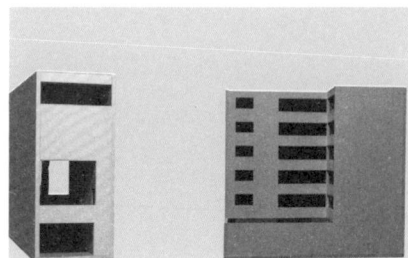

Tomas Cabral, Miguel Lopo de Carvalho

Olivia Linder, Nathalie Oren p28

Camilla Carli, Thomas Cianflone p32-33

Chiara Zunino p26-27

Marco Craveiro Leite Velho, Diogo Rabaça Figueiredo p29

Eleonora Dalcher, Anne-Dorothée Herbort p34

Andrea Scotti p35

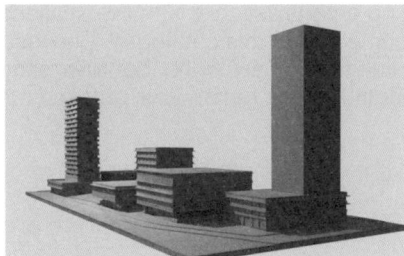
Niccolò Cozzi, Luciana Diaz p38-39

Marta Bardelli, Florence Harbach

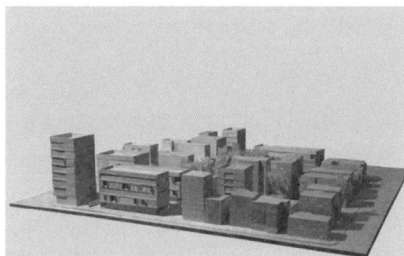
Alexandra De la Chapelle, Sofia Travassos p31

Marella Carboni, Nicoletta Caputo p30

Acknowledgements

The work we undertook over the Autumn semester 2010 was made possible by the support and collaboration of many parties.

I am particularly indebted to Peter Keinan for his help in the preparation of the briefing documents and the support he offered. The guidance he gave the students during our time in Israel were exceptionally generous, and his presence at the final reviews and careful critique of the projects proved invaluable.

I would also like to thank Rosamund Diamond, Lidor Shalit and Stefan Davidovici for their precious contribution to the reviews, and Jeremie Hoffman and Sergio Lehrman for their support and assistance during our visit to Tel Aviv.

As always, I am grateful to my assistants Georg Nickisch, Sarah Maunder and Marina Aldrovandi for their dedication, professionalism and good humour, and to Corinne Weber for her assistance in producing this catalogue.

Finally, any semester stands or falls on the work of the students, and I would like to thank all of them for engaging enthusiastically with the challenges of the brief and producing the projects documented in this catalogue. The issues they attempted to grapple with are not amenable to easy solutions, but their seriousness in embracing the responsibilities of architecture was remarkable and is a credit to them all.

Credits
Concept: Jonathan Sergison
Editing: Marina Aldrovandi
Graphic concept: Cartlidge Levene
Graphic design: Sarah Maunder, Corinne Weber
Printing: Publistampa, Italy
Paper: Munken Pure

Copyright © 2014 Studio Sergison, Accademia di architettura, Università della Svizzera italiana, Mendrisio

To order a copy of this publication, please contact: marinaaldrovandi@sergisonbates.co.uk

ISBN 978-0-9542371-8-9

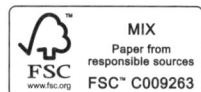

MIX
Paper from responsible sources
FSC
www.fsc.org
FSC™ C009263

Università della Svizzera italiana

Accademia di architettura